D1222310

JAN - - 2016

CHARLESTON COUNTY LIBRARY

A20332 236141

CHARLESTON COUNTY LIBRARY

CHARLESTON COUNTY LIBRARY

Apatosaurus

by Charles Lennie

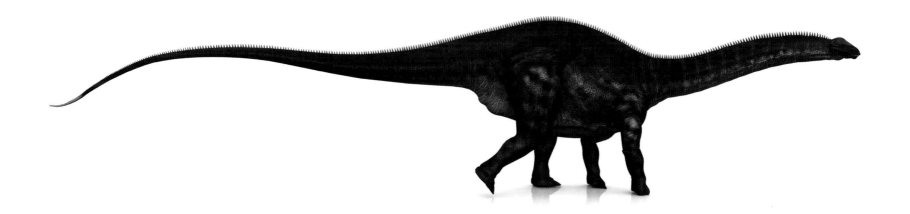

WITHDRAWN

ABDO
DINOSAURS
Kids

www.abdopublishing.com

Published by Abdo Kids, a division of ABDO, PO Box 398166, Minneapolis, Minnesota 55439.

Copyright © 2015 by Abdo Consulting Group, Inc. International copyrights reserved in all countries. No part of this book may be reproduced in any form without written permission from the publisher.

Printed in the United States of America, North Mankato, Minnesota.

052014

092014

 **THIS BOOK CONTAINS RECYCLED MATERIALS**

Photo Credits: AP Images, Corbis, Getty Images, Minnesota Zoo (mnzoo.org), Shutterstock, Thinkstock, © Eduard Solà Vázquez / CC-BY-SA-3.0 p.21, © User:Ghedoghedo / CC-BY-SA-3.0 p.21

Production Contributors: Teddy Borth, Jennie Forsberg, Grace Hansen

Design Contributors: Candice Keimig, Laura Rask, Dorothy Toth

Library of Congress Control Number: 2013952310

Cataloging-in-Publication Data

Lennie, Charles.

 Apatosaurus / Charles Lennie.

  p. cm. -- (Dinosaurs)

ISBN 978-1-62970-022-9 (lib. bdg.)

Includes bibliographical references and index.

1. Apatosaurus--Juvenile literature.   I. Title.

567.913--dc23

                    2013952310

Table of Contents

Apatosaurus

The Apatosaurus lived
a long time ago. It lived
about 150 million years ago.

The Apatosaurus was a gentle giant. It is one of the largest animals to have walked the earth.

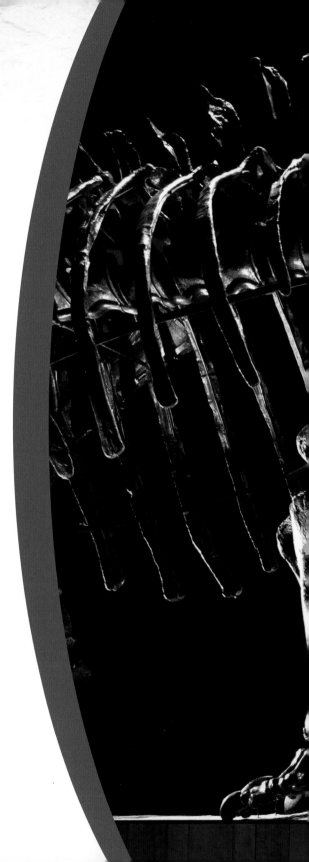

The Apatosaurus had a
very long neck. It could
reach leaves high in the trees.

9

The Apatosaurus had a very long tail. Its tail helped it to balance.

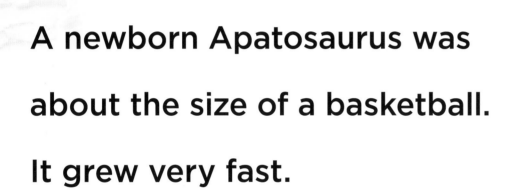

A newborn Apatosaurus was about the size of a basketball. It grew very fast.

The Apatosaurus grew to be 75 feet (23 m) long. It weighed more than five adult elephants!

The Apatosaurus had **nostrils** on top of its head. Its nostrils may have acted like a **snorkel** while swimming.

17

Food

The Apatosaurus ate plants. It had skinny teeth that were shaped like pencils.

Fossils

Apatosaurus **fossils** have been found throughout the United States.

Wyoming

Utah

Colorado

Oklahoma

21

More Facts

- The Apatosaurus laid large eggs. One egg was likely up to 1 foot (30 cm) wide. An Apatosaurus egg was shaped like a football.

- The Apatosaurus swallowed leaves. It swallowed stones to help grind up the leaves in its stomach.

- The Apatosaurus could eat 500 pounds (226 kg) of food each day.

- The Apatosaurus was mistakenly called a Brontosaurus.

Glossary

balance – to keep from falling over.

fossils – the remains of a once living thing; could be a footprint or skeleton.

nostrils – openings in the nose that allow you to breathe.

snorkel – a tube that allows you to breathe while you are underwater.

Index

abdokids.com

Use this code to log on to abdokids.com and access crafts, games, videos and more!

Abdo Kids Code:
DAK0229